BURNING

OF

ABSENCE

BURNING OF ABSENCE
Jessica Thiru

QUERENCIA

Querencia Press – Chicago Il

QUERENCIA PRESS

© Copyright 2025
Jessica Thiru

ISBN 978 1 963943 42 9

www.querenciapress.com

First Published in 2025

Querencia Press, LLC
Chicago IL

Printed & Bound in the United States of America

For grief that names itself survival.
For the places that remember me long after my leaving.

The world is happening in a room that I can't enter,
life is happening in a gathering I am not invited to.
Being unwanted is a language I am fluent in.

—Fatima Aamer Bilal

How do we forgive ourselves for all of the things we
did not become?

—Doc Luben

CONTENTS

1.

My body is burning with the shame of not belonging,
  my body is longing.
    I am the sin of memory and the absence of memory.

—Warsan Shire

I still want to tell the story: how our waiting hung like a burning fog in the room. How the IV drip became something sharp etching away at our subtleties. We gave grief our hands, our lips, but it wanted the body. Wanted all there is to know about blood. About taking.

I held his hand and felt knives running through him. I held his hand and the room turned an uninviting hue. The truth is, love is an anarchy we don't mind. Sickness doesn't ask for permission. Doesn't say goodbye when leaving after taking what it came for. Goodbye, by which I mean *sorry*. What it came for, by which I mean *who*. Then, that room in the corner of the hospital became the edge of the world. Became restless with its own becoming: straining under the weight of unlikely possibility. Bruised against odds.

His eyes shut quiet. Silence is only ever a beautiful language when eyes meet; when two hands become ten fingers, naked and warm against each other. What else is silence but bad news. Something wonderful lost in translation of now.

When I still believed in god, I grieved, mostly because I was taught someone like him would go to hell. And I felt sinful for wondering why I was exempt from it: the endless burning of flesh. The crying that can be heard by archangels but not by humans. Not by me. I grieve now because his laughter remains a wave of something I cannot run my fingers through. Because his date of death will always be 5 days before his daughter's date of birth, regardless of time and its passing. I grieve with no hands and no lips, but my godlessness lets me mourn a second time.

JUSTICE IS JUST A PRIVILEGE

To all the bodies buried before their time,
bodies of innocent women
that have been hushed beneath the soil.
The men of this country fought to keep you quiet
and now the earth has no choice but to make you silent,
a tribute to you all.

To all the women
who have envisioned their death countless times
imagined every scenario possible
where every bone in your body will have to learn survival,
fighting against ~~someone~~ who is fighting for
what's between your thighs
where your body will be left abandoned
and your eyes dry after crying tears you never knew you had.

I'm sorry that you've had to prepare yourself
for a battle that should never take place.

That you've had to fear not being fearful
because not fearing the fear you're supposed to feel
is asking for it.
I'm sorry that it's not safe to think it's safe anymore
that there is no square inch of this country that fights to save you,
no law truly there to guard you
and so, instead, you have to keep your guard up.
Knowing that if you ever let yourself be without a care,
if you ever accidentally separate yourself from victimhood
the blame will still be yours.

Even if you've kept up the battle every day since
you've known that being a woman means that any moment you
         could be a no one.

To all the bodies buried before their time
trapped inside a casket of traumatized flesh
scared to live outside of your existence.
Prepared for the day when a ~~man~~ might
consume your body down to crumbs
leave your heart a home to heartache
even when you've prepared it for the day
you envisioned, where a ~~man~~ may
take what he believes belongs to ~~him~~.
The day where you would find strength in feeling weak
grateful to be left being able to feel anything.

I'm sorry that you've had to prepare yourself for premature death.
You've had to make peace with dying in pieces.
You've been taught to dream and aspire to be something
but a man can reduce you to less than the ground ~~he~~ walks on
leave your body a lost cause
because he thinks your body's only purpose is to be at ~~his~~ service.
You've had to be okay with the fact that even then,
justice is not something you're entitled to.
Justice is just a privilege in this country
and you'd be lucky if your absence was acknowledged

because as you are, your presence never is.

in my mother's family to be married is to be silent. mom understood this well. at just 25 she fit herself like a phantom beneath my father's tongue. spoke only as a reverberation of him. a year later she had my father's first child. allowed herself to be swallowed, dreams first, by the child she carried. we haven't found her since. 18 years later, her mother, too, was swallowed by a gluttonous cancer. we prayed, but god let her burn like a forsaken aftermath. holy chaff is all that remained. I predict she still haunts her own body.

There is nothing that can satiate a man's hunger, I promise you.
A man's thirst is that of a battlefield after war still craving blood.
Trust me, I'm telling the truth.
I come from a long line of women who've tasted their own blood
by a man's will.
A long line of women who survived on their own flesh
by a man's will.

i

        my father beat my mother to the breast. my
brother told me the stories of how she would squeal at
his wrath like stranded prey at the mercy of a beast. my
brother told me he would try hide but my father's
footsteps would send darkness running, bare boned,
into the night. I too witnessed the violence. once, after
having been beaten breathless, my mother resurrected
from their room, her face, darker than sin, crying louder
than the belt that made her body weep. after moving in
with my father, her mouth became an open field with
gates. because what's a marriage if a man isn't telling
you to *shut the fuck up, you stupid brainless bird! shut*
the fuck up! become subservient. shrink. you can say
anything you want but it doesn't leave your polluted
mouth, you dumb fucking bird.

ii

        once, at my now dead uncle's house, a man
hammered a beer bottle into his wife's cheek. left her
face distorted like an heirloom photograph. we couldn't
recognize her no matter how hard we squinted. the

house was baptized in fear. peace averted. my cousins
and I tried to hide but darkness went running, bare
boned, into the night. is that what a man's wrath does?
sends darkness elsewhere with its teeth chattering. we
were taken like livestock to another uncle's house. even
now, I remember how our mouths were dry from prayer.
I bet our bodies, swollen with apprehension, quivered
throughout the night recalling that wicked scene.

There is nothing that you can do
that will satiate a man's hunger, I promise you.
Believe me, I'm telling you the truth.
I come from a long line of women whose skin
became a casket once a man touched them.

FEAR OF VOICEMAIL
a series of journal entries
—*after Imani Cezanne*

Wednesday, August 16, 2021.

My little sister is *really* a little sister. She has one and a half rows of teeth. She loves fast food on a Friday after school. She's the kind of girl that's there for everyone but never there for herself. She has the type of smile that makes her eyes shine so bright you'd swear the sun looks up to her, or into her, or sees itself in her. She's yet to learn the world is like barbed wire against the kindness of girls still learning fractions. She still believes in the goodness of strangers and...*she always answers the phone.*

I called my sister today just because I could, and because she's still alive. On the other end of the dial tone, I longed for a voice in the shape of her. In the wait, I yielded to my own need to escape a reality I did not consent to. Maybe there is no eloquent way to describe wanting a loved one to stay breathing. I sat on the other side of '*the number you are trying to call is not reachable*'. I tried to remain someone she would be proud of. Asked myself questions I already knew the answers to: Will her corpse live to tell the story of an attempt living as a woman? Will the scars on her flesh awake the activist in you? Her bones, one too many to just be a photo with the caption 'rest in peace' but not enough to let women live in it. Will we promise to never forget her? Or will we promise to make noise before we allow ourselves to? Will she be another reason for you to act like an activist but never be the *act* in action that really makes you one? Will we speak about how she looked when she smiled? How we saw the sun in her eyes when she did? Will we talk about how brave she was to go on about her life? As if death as a woman in this country is not nearly inevitable. Will we speak about how her name found any room left on your tongue *to roll off like a hashtag,* as if there aren't hundreds fighting for space and thousands fighting to be recognized? Would you know how she was silenced, *but never how her voice sounded? I called my sister today just because I could...and because...I'm still alive.*

This was the most noise I could make.

Thursday 17

Yesterday the best I did was not recoil. I let the dial tone be a sound instead of a metaphor. Walked through the long dark throat of legislation. Wondered, *how civil a disobedience do you expect* when women are assaulted and then murdered, and a man remains un-sentenced? If there is a place where a dial tone isn't a corridor for grief how many women does it cost to get there?

Yesterday I got tired of kindly trying to attack men's egos. Yesterday I got tired of trying to explain that there is no correlation between assault and a woman's clothing because fully dressed or not, a man will still see what he wants to see. *Yesterday I was an activist. Today, I'm just a big sister.*

Today the fight in me is losing the will to fight with me—or to fight for me if need be. *Meanwhile the streets are gagging on the flesh of the slaughtered. They do not chew with their mouths closed. There is nothing polite about a buffet of dead women's bodies.*

Men are already at the top of the food chain. All we can hope for is an exit not a hierarchy, but men would rather be the bodyguards of their ego, instead of fighting to help guard our bodies. This is the remnant:

> —*the number you are trying to call is not reachable*

> No one on the other side of your waiting

> A food chain built almost entirely of women's bodies

> Too much uncertainty for such a certain grave

~~The police will pick up the pieces.~~ The police will ask about what we were wearing, but I don't know why we're allowed to speak if our words are equivalent to silence. Since the clothes we wear speak louder than the words that leave our mouths, with the little authority we think we have—which clearly isn't enough to have a say over our own bodies.

The police will ask about what we were wearing as if there's a grey area between our dignity and saying *no*, but I know for a fact that they could kill my sister today. Just because she's a woman, and because she's still alive. *The number you are trying to call is not—*

This is my most reasonable fear.

*italicized lines are taken or adapted from the spoken word piece
'Protest" by Imani Cezanne

PORTRAIT OF GIRLHOOD AS A DOOR TO GODHOOD

Someone once asked me,
"Why not choose forgiveness over violence?"
I asked, "Which one came first?"

Some things I could have never prepared for
    Last winter—the inaudible parts of me that survived its
stillness.

    The brush of seasons against each other newly discovered
by sadness.
    The way the sky stretched itself after I no longer believed in
heaven.

When I was 17, I thought I could escape home without the scent
of memory.
And for a while I did. But my knowing slipped out of itself.

Now at 19, I am still haunted by unshakable cruelties
    The parts of my mother's girlhood I failed to rescue.
    How I thought myself indestructible and then destroyed
myself.

*Who could have prepared me for my own lack of mercy? Or the
world and its teeth?*

This is the answer:
On the seventh day god rested
And on the eighth day god chose violence.

2.

Quarantined in a bad dream

—Phoebe Bridgers

I set the house on fire. Remember, word for word,
           the story of my father's boyhood but forget my first name.
    The choice to run from home was always
mine but no place was far enough to escape my father's hands.
    So there I was—fluent in aching. Bones watered down.
                     A fist's worth of gasoline on the tongue.
Secrets luminous and swelling at my core like a burning star. No
           version of this memory has an exit.

It was hot. The shed filled with the stench of day-old sweat.
               The insides of my mouth
        cut from my own thirst. What was strange was not my
    reflection through the broken mirror, but how I noticed
    it wouldn't move. Then I heard it—his voice. The way he said
           my name like a
    prayer. Every syllable, delicate like
something holy, like something he would not let learn the ground.
              The authority in it carried me to the next
  room. He looked at me. Each pupil, the size of a muzzle I had to
    fit through if
        I wanted to survive.
The girl, a few blinks beneath him—her hair, thick, falling like a broken
           promise. Her face, a sound for no one to hear.
               The sun then, almost a black pit.
        Moments of light still sharpening
           dusk before the night sealed.

FAMILY KITCHEN

Hate has the outline of a man I was once fond of
& I can't unlearn it.

A body dead on a tiled floor is still a loud experience. What would
you call it?

Sometimes what happens in family kitchens anywhere else we
refer to as hell.

If you kill someone twice which version of them is remembered
by your hands. Which version of them leaves you an animal in
the dark hunting for something more than forgiveness.

Outside it's 6am and birds gently wake up the suburb. Inside, I
don't know which hour hosts this kind of evil. Blood piles on the
floor, and the kitchen smells like ripened dread.

Home is a soft word for secret. Dagger a synonym for thunder.
Here on earth, his shame is also a fire only a stranger's smile
could suffocate. The best explanation for all of this: very little
happens for a reason. A prayer in any language would fall short
of mercy.

REPENTANCE, THE DECREPIT THING

my father's screaming caught my legs
      like a bird's neck between a curious child's hands
it felt like I was running backwards
      into the mouth of a shore
my lungs almost overflowing with salt water
every bone in my body
      a worn out mercy
my father's screaming stained my ears with something best
      described as
      my mother's sorrow.

the boy wailing from my father's terror stood, still
      alive but dying, naked in indecency.
his bleeding—a decrepit thing.
I knelt at his feet like I was praying
      a futile prayer
having been shunned from faith by faith itself.

even in my sleep my heart hung around my neck
      like a swaying pendant.
there's a type of hell in my throat
      I don't want to discover
the way it held my tears down
      with no hands
(even in my sleep).

how come I feel most when dreaming?

If lack of love is a sin
      god, how we need forgiveness

I've never really understood repentance
        but I feel I've grown hungry for it
    we all have.

i love anything until it hates me. you would know this.
      still. i conclude my days the same way:
trying to make sense of our abrupt ending.
                but think of a fist.
consider all it's yet to ruin with its touch:
      a pure white wall. a face's symmetry. a marriage.
                    consider.
it's a usual 5pm in our hometown. you know, you don't notice the
      dogs barking until they stop.
the sunset wakes a dead room in the house, it's sudden music.
                still.
      there's only so many texts i can send you before i want to eat
      my own hands.
every apology replays itself in my sleep, like a voice from a radio
      you can hear even long after it's been turned off.
              you know, when your head
becomes the radio. you, the drawn-out drive.
      i shut my eyes hard enough hoping they're swallowed by my
      skull,
              and still. it's you.
every dream with your face becomes murder.
      becomes a memory that thinks itself a film.
even in dreams i say sorry so often my jaw bends backwards
            and all that's left are:
very tiny limbs glued together. the ugliest parts of a beautiful city. the
      fingernails of
      everyone that's ever lived, and i know.
            i've pushed you away.
this is the only phenomenon: one always finds it easier to leave.

ABANDONED LETTERS OR CONFESSIONS SINCE COLLEGE

1

I've started getting night terrors again.

2

My mom flew off to America. We haven't
spoken since. I pick up the phone to call her
and my throat becomes a loaded gun underwater.
So instead I don't pick up the phone. I mean
I pick it up but not to call her. Not to see
how she's doing or if she's eaten and if she's
happy; not to ask her how the weather there
is like.

3

I stopped wearing my retainers.
Fuck the retainers.

4

When I first left home for college
I couldn't bring myself to tell my mom I missed
her cooking. Missed the bond we never shared and
conversations that were never spoken. Missed hearing
her distant voice from my room whilst she was on a
phone call and all the ways it sounded like a Sunday.

5

How do I miss someone that's made me feel
unwanted my whole life?
How do I miss someone that never let me love them?

6

Look at what all this relation, all this blood has
done. Look at how we suffer from forced
belonging.

7

My sister is 15 now, the same age I was when
self- loathing took over me. I wish I could
shield her from what the world does to one
at that age: unzips the spine and fills you
with a permanent ugliness only you can see.
I want to protect her from the world without
her having to leave it.

8

Loneliness is an echo heard only by those
who have felt its stillness. I think my mother
and I share the same loneliness. She left the
air in the house screaming in falsetto.
I hear it because I know the feeling. The way
it feels to be around bodies that are just bodies.
The way it feels to smile without the eyes losing
territory on the face, not moved by skin.

9

I sometimes fear what lack of love as
a child has made me. I fear more what
it hasn't.

10

Every city I've learnt to call
home has spat me out and set me
alight. It's crippling how nothing wants
me. Not even where I come from.

11

I don't think I've ever been loved the way I love.
I will never be sure of this. Unfortunately,
that's how vulnerability works.

12

The way we heal from things we
don't exactly remember doesn't
make the healing any easier.

13

Thank you for loving me, friend.
It made me feel alive again.

it's funny in an obscure way how the cosmos
saturated with blinking stars
and other-worldly things still produces
silence. awkward stillness.
at 17, once I figured out I was just another
one of the universe's grudges with mortality,
the universe did seem insincere.
offering so much space without telling me
exactly how to make use of it.
yet even in its unfairness
I still have a feral hunger
for my own tender human experience. and yes.

I could imagine roaming my whole life
alone under lustful moonlight.
not because of all the ways it could be romantic
and how loneliness can sometimes sound
purposeful on the tongue.
but because there's something almost
beautiful about no one knowing my name
maybe more than a handful of decades from now;
something about being forgotten as just
another knot in time.

every time i'm walking alone in the city everyone
feels familiar as if we've
cried together in someplace that melts on the tongue
like an afterlife or i've
eaten their mom's food on a Tuesday.
both of which are miracles i never
want to get used to. the truth: i never
planned on staying here this long.
which is not to say i've hated
my entire existence but since i crawled out of
childhood my aliveness has been far less forgivable.
to this day, leftovers
of dusk dance in my childhood bedroom trying
to drown out whatever woe
i left behind. the truth: memory has only ever been a burden.
has only ever left me with a want big enough
it could give me purpose
if i let it. i'm always fantasizing the end. My
insides shutting down like a
voluntary apocalypse. the sky feels further than usual
these days though
i don't ask why, and every so often i wonder
how many lives i could live
at once if nostalgia let me.

THANKS

This book is a full circle moment for me and I'm immeasurably grateful to anyone who ever gave me feedback, encouraged me, and prompted me with ideas. Thank you for beckoning my then creativity with your patience and care.

A special thanks to my dear friend, Azraa Slamong for being my biggest support throughout the years. Thank you for remaining sincere and honest towards me and my writing. I'm not sure I would be doing this if you weren't who you are to me.

Thank you to my sister Ruby, for being. I don't have a grand enough expression of my gratitude towards you. You're the best sister anyone could have. Thank you for your unwavering support.

Thank you to Emily Perkovich for believing in this chapbook enough to bring it into the world.

Thank you to 29 Brodigan Street and South Africa for molding me. I miss your winter afternoons.

To the reader, these words are yours now. Thank you for holding them.

And to younger me who dreamed of this so much she barely believed it—thank you for enduring.

ACKNOWLEDGMENTS

repentance, the decrepit thing was first published in Scavengers Literary Magazine

brutal philia was first published in "Not Ghosts, But Spirits IV" (Querencia Press)